WORLD WAR II

John Perritano

Created by Q2AMedia

www.q2amedia.com

Text, design & illustrations Copyright © Leopard Learning 2009

Editor Jessica Cohn
Publishing Director Chester Fisher
Client Service Manager Sujatha Menon
Project Manager Kumar Kunal
Art Director Joita Das
Designer Parul Gambhir
Picture Researcher Debarata Sen and Anju Pathak

Tangerine Press edition © 2010 Scholastic Inc.

an imprint of
SCHOLASTIC
www.scholastic.com

Scholastic and Tangerine Press and associated logos are trademarks of Scholastic Inc.

Published by Tangerine Press, an imprint of Scholastic Inc.,

557 Broadway; New York, NY 10012

10 9 8 7 6 5 4 3 2 1

ISBN: 978-0-545-24947-8

Printed and bound in Shenzhen, China

Contents

Path to War

World War I (1914–1918) took the lives of millions of people. It was one of the deadliest wars in history. Some nations disappeared, and new countries rose from the remains.

The First World War was called the "War to End All Wars." Yet, the First World War sowed the seeds for an even greater conflict—the Second World War. In World War II, Germany, Italy, and Japan fought the Allied powers, which included Great Britain, the Soviet Union, and the United States. World War II involved most of the world's nations.

Death and Destruction

World War II (1939–1945) was a deadly war. The new weapons of World War II included the devastating atomic bomb. During World War II, about 25 million soldiers died. Perhaps twice as many civilians were killed. The Allies won in the end. Yet, much of Europe was damaged or destroyed.

The fighting left Stalingrad (a Soviet city) and Berlin (Germany's capital) in ruins. Hiroshima and Nagasaki (Japanese cities) were destroyed by atomic bombs.

▶ U.S. troops fight in a German town square in 1945.

German Panzers move through Poland.

Versailles

The Second World War began about 20 years after the end of the First World War. How could the world fight another war so soon? Part of the answer has to do with the Treaty of Versailles, the peace agreement that ended World War I in 1918.

The treaty got its name because officials from the warring nations met in Versailles, France. Most officials who signed the treaty wanted lasting peace. However, some Allied leaders wanted to punish the Germans for waging such a costly and destructive war.

German soldiers march in Czechoslovakia in 1939.

The Payback

The treaty made Germany solely responsible for the war and forced the Germans to pay billions of dollars in **reparations** to the Allied nations for war damages. "This is not peace. It is an **armistice** for 20 years," predicted Ferdinand Foch, the Allied commander and marshal of France.

Young Hitler

Germany's colonies around the world were given to Belgium, France, the United Kingdom, and Japan. About 3 million German-speaking people were made part of a new country called Czechoslovakia. The treaty angered many Germans, including a young soldier named Adolf Hitler. Hitler had served as a German corporal during World War I.

Hitler believed that his country had been stabbed in the back by its own government. He vowed to return the German Fatherland to its former glory.

▲ Nazi troops parade for Hitler in 1935.

Hitler's Rise

Adolf Hitler was born in Austria in 1889. He was the son of a customs official. Hitler dropped out of high school when he was 16. In 1920, he joined the National Socialist German Workers' Party, which later became known as the Nazi Party. In 1923, Hitler attempted to overthrow the German government. This plan failed, and Hitler was imprisoned.

While in prison, Hitler wrote a book called *Mein Kampf*, or *My Struggle*, which laid out his plans for the future. When freed in December 1924, he began rebuilding the Nazi Party. In the 1930s, economic troubles, known as the Great Depression, hit Germany as well as the rest of the world. Millions of Germans were out of work. Hitler's speeches inspired the broken nation.

In the 1930s, the Nazis won seats in the German parliament, or Reichstag. In 1933, Hitler was named Germany's chancellor. A few months later Hitler declared that the Nazis were the only political party, and he became a dictator. The iron fist of Hitler came smashing down.

▶ In 1928, Hitler is pictured at a Nazi rally.

In the concentration camps, many prisoners starved.

The Holocaust, Beginnings

The Holocaust is the name given to the abuse and murder of the Jewish people that took place in Germany under the Nazis. Hitler blamed the Jews and Communists for Germany's problems. He declared the Aryan race to be special.

Who was Aryan? The Nazis believed white people of Northern European heritage to be Aryans. They considered other kinds of people to be inferior. This way of thinking made it easier for the German government to pass **repressive** laws against the Jews. Jewish Germans could not hold certain jobs. The Nazis seized Jewish property and businesses and walled off Jews in "ghettos."

November 9, 1938 was *Kristallnacht,* or "night of broken glass." Nazi storm troopers and others raided Jewish businesses. Nearly 100 Jews were beaten to death. Hundreds more were injured. Thousands of businesses and more than 1,000 synagogues were destroyed. The streets were littered with broken glass.

Hitler created concentration camps to secretly put into effect what he called "the final solution of the Jewish question." Several of the camps were located in places that were easy to get to by roads or railways. A large number of Jews were sent to these camps between 1942 and 1944.

Japan and Italy

Japan was trying to take over its side of the world. By the mid-1930s, Japan had changed from an isolated country into an industrial powerhouse. Yet, Japan had few natural resources of its own. The island nation had to depend on imports from other countries, especially oil from the United States.

Many Japanese politicians and members of the military wanted to be free of Western influence. To gain independence, the Japanese tried to force their neighbors into a "Co-Prosperity Sphere." Within this sphere, Japan would be able to take the raw materials it needed, including oil.

In 1931, Japan invaded the Chinese province of Manchuria. A small battle between the Japanese army and Chinese troops took place. A full invasion of China followed.

Key Events

MANCHURIA

JAPAN

CHINA

FRENCH INDO-CHINA

PHILIPPINES

BRITISH MALAYA

NETHERLANDS EAST INDIES

Pacific Ocean

0 200 400 600 800
km

- **Japanese Occupation of East Asia**

Japanese Empire (prior to 1930)

Occupied by 1932

Occupied by 1937

Occupied by 1938

Occupied by 1942

Italy Flexes Its Muscles

During the 1930s, Italy was also acting aggressively. In 1935, Italy invaded the African nation of Ethiopia. Italy's leader, Benito Mussolini, planned to build an empire like the one created by the ancient Romans. Mussolini wanted his "New Roman Empire" to stretch from the Middle East to Africa. In April 1939, Italy took over Albania. Mussolini also wanted to **annex** Malta, Corsica, and Tunisia.

▲ Benito Mussolini salutes his troops in Rome in 1933.

◄ Italian troops are on the move in northern Africa in 1935.

11

Germany Rising

Adolf Hitler ignored the rules of the Treaty of Versailles. He worked to rebuild Germany's military. He killed or imprisoned anyone in his country who opposed him. He sent millions of Jews and other targeted people to concentration camps, where they worked for the war effort or were killed. The German leader made friends with Mussolini. Germany and Italy formed the Rome-Berlin Axis. The Axis powers would later include Japan.

In March 1938, Hitler invaded Austria, Germany's neighbor. He succeeded in merging Austria with Germany. The German leader also wanted to rule the Sudetenland, an area in Czechoslovakia where German was spoken. Neville Chamberlain, the British prime minister, knew about Hitler's plans. Chamberlain feared a deadly repeat of World War I. He looked for a **compromise** in order to avoid another war.

▶ Nazis march in Czechoslovakia.

Appeasement

In September 1938, Chamberlain went to Germany to meet with Hitler. British and German officials reached an agreement on the Sudetenland. Chamberlain returned home, declaring that he had achieved "peace in our time."

After that meeting, Britain and France told Czechoslovakia that neither major power would stop Germany if Hitler took over the Sudetenland. Yet, that policy, known as **appeasement**, made Hitler bolder. Hitler's troops marched into Bohemia, Moravia, and Slovakia. Poland seemed to be next on his list of targets. By the end of March 1939, the British and French were fed up. They vowed to defend Poland if the Germans attacked. Europe once again appeared to be heading toward war.

▲ Neville Chamberlain and Adolf Hitler meet in 1938.

Blitzkrieg

In the summer of 1939, the people of Poland feared a German invasion. The Poles were tough fighters with an army of 1 million. Yet, they were no match for the mighty German army and air force. Polish leaders decided that, should Germany attack, they would fight as long as possible, hoping that Britain and France would come to their aid.

On September 1, 1939, Germany swept into Poland by air and land in a surprise attack. The Germans called it *blitzkrieg*, or 'lightning war'. Germany headed across the Polish border with more than 2,000 tanks and 1,000 planes. The Germans smashed Poland's defenses. The German air force, the Luftwaffe, destroyed much of Poland's air force while many Polish planes were still on the ground.

▶ Newspapers around the world cover the Nazis' movements.

The War Machine

Britain and France declared war on Germany two days later. Unfortunately, neither country was in a position to face the German **juggernaut**, or unstoppable force. Britain did not have enough troops, but its aircraft went after German combat forces as they advanced through the Polish countryside. The French made plans to defend their homeland based on their Maginot Line, defensive fortifications that had been built in eastern France near the German border before the war.

▼ Germany invades Poland in September 1939.

Help from the Soviets

Poland surrendered on September 28, 1939. The Soviet Union secretly had signed an **alliance** with Germany before the invasion. Soviet troops took over the eastern part of Poland, imprisoning thousands of people, including Polish soldiers.

With Poland now in Nazi hands, Hitler dangled the idea of peace to the Allies. But he did not really want to settle Germany's differences with Britain and France. Hitler just wanted time for his army to rest and gain strength. He secretly planned to march against Belgium, the Netherlands, and France. His peace offering lured many in those nations into a false sense of security.

Nazi Advance

As the Nazis turned their attention to Western Europe, the British sent a small defensive force to France to slow down the Germans. In April 1940, Germany invaded Denmark and Norway. In May of that year, the Germans quickly conquered Belgium, the Netherlands, and Luxembourg.

▲ People in Paris weep openly when the Nazis arrive.

Onward March

Germany raced toward the English Channel. The Germans successfully cut through the middle of the British and French forces. Winston Churchill, Britain's new prime minister, tried to control the situation.

Backs to the Water

By late May 1940, German forces had trapped thousands of British and French soldiers near Dunkirk, a seaport in northern France. The French and British had nowhere to go. Their backs were to the English Channel.

▼ Allied ships rescue Allies stranded at Dunkirk.

Dunkirk

At Dunkirk, food and supplies ran low as the Allies waited for the advancing German army to crush them. Then, Hitler made a major mistake. He ordered his tank crews to halt their advance.

Instead of having his Panzers, or German battle tanks, finish off the French and British troops at Dunkirk, Hitler directed the Luftwaffe to destroy the Allies. Yet, his air force could not do the job. By the time the Nazi tanks started moving once again, heavy rain had made the attack more difficult. This gave the Allies the chance they needed to rescue stranded troops at Dunkirk.

▼ British and French soldiers are rescued from Dunkirk in 1940.

● Rescue at Dunkirk (1940)

1 By late May, the German army had trapped the Allies at the port city of Dunkirk.

2 On May 26th, the British Admiralty launched Operation Dynamo, the plan to evacuate the Allies from Dunkirk by sea. The 10-day operation saved hundreds of thousands of soldiers. British Prime Minister Winston Churchill said his forces would never surrender.

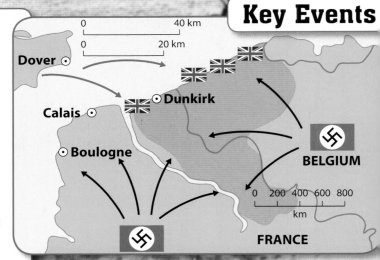

Key Events

0 — 40 km
0 — 20 km

Dover ⊙

Calais ⊙

Dunkirk

⊙ Boulogne

BELGIUM

0 200 400 600 800
km

FRANCE

Belgium, the Netherlands, and Luxembourg were now under German control. Paris was within Hitler's grasp. On June 14th, the Nazi troops marched into Paris. Two days later, French Prime Minister Paul Reynaud resigned. Deputy Prime Minister Phillippe Petain, a hero of World War I, took over the French government. He moved it from Paris to Vichy and called for an immediate truce with Germany.

▲ The Nazis take control of the French capital.

"We Must Stop Fighting"

On June 17th, Petain went on the radio. He told the French people, "It is with a heavy heart that I tell you today that we must stop fighting." The French signed surrender documents in the same railway car where the Germans had surrendered in World War I. Petain worked closely with the German occupation forces and established the French State.

Battle of Britain

Hitler began plans to invade Great Britain. Hitler's first step was to send in forces to try to control the air around the island nation. Then, the Nazis would start an invasion by sea. In July 1940, the German air attack began. The bombings and air battles that followed became known as the Battle of Britain.

German aircraft heavily bombed British factories and airfields in southern England. Then, Hitler ordered bombing to begin on English cities, including London. British fighter pilots fought back by bombing Berlin, Germany. By mid-September, the Germans had lost many planes and pilots. Hitler postponed the invasion, bringing the bombing of Britain to an end.

Ernie Pyle was an American newspaper reporter based in London. He reported how well the British people endured the German bombing. "It isn't flag-waving," he said. "It is simply a quaint old British idea that nobody is going to push them around."

▶ Fire rescue workers extinguish flames in London in 1941.

Holding off the Tide

President Franklin Roosevelt pushed the United States to give Britain 50 old **destroyers**. In return, Britain gave the U.S. some military bases in the Caribbean and Canada. The U.S. Congress passed the Lend-Lease Act, which provided Great Britain with desperately needed military supplies. Great Britain agreed to repay America after the war.

America Watches

Americans listened to the news of the growing war with concern. The people who did not want the United States to become involved spoke out. The United States was suffering from economic problems during the Great Depression and was officially **neutral**. Yet, President Franklin Roosevelt could see that Great Britain needed America's help to survive.

▼ The war continues to grab the headlines.

er **Daily Enterprise.**

TWO CENTS

Weather

TER, MASS., TUESDAY, SEPTEMBER 10, 1940

NAZI PLANES DROP HEAVY BOMBS IN THIRD ATTACK

MEETING OF MERCHANTS IS CONDUCTED

Action Taken By Group On Continuing Wednesday Closings

CLASS COURSE

Instruction Favored By Merchants Attending Meeting

London Apartment Blasted By Nazi Bombs

MISSILES OF 800 TO 1000 POUNDS USED

Dropped Near St. Paul's, Guild Hall and Bank Of England

BRITISH STRIKE

Fliers Carry Out 45-Minute Raid In Air Drive On Berlin

Operation Barbarossa

On June 22, 1941, Germany broke its peace agreement with the Soviet Union. Three million German soldiers attacked the Soviet Union, using thousands of tanks, aircraft, and artillery pieces. The fighting broke out along a front that was 2,000 miles (3,219 kilometers) long. The Germans code-named the attack "Barbarossa," in honor of Emperor Frederick I Barbarossa, who ruled Germany during the Middle Ages.

"We have only to kick in the door, and the whole rotten structure will come crashing down," Hitler boasted. The Nazis swept through the Soviet Union as they had in Poland, Belgium, the Netherlands, Luxembourg, and France. The Germans would fight the Soviets for four years. Hitler wanted to eliminate the threat of Communism.

◀ Russian soldiers prepare to fight German soldiers.

Stalingrad

By the spring of 1942, the Germans were outside Stalingrad, an important industrial city on the Volga River. Stalingrad was named for Soviet leader Joseph Stalin. The city was the gateway to the oil-rich Caucasus region.

Nazis attack a Soviet village in 1941.

From Building to Building

By capturing Stalingrad, the Nazis hoped to capture much-needed oil to fuel their tanks, airplanes, and other war machines. They pushed toward the city in June and early July. The Soviets defended their city, fighting the Germans in the streets and buildings. By the beginning of November, Stalingrad was in ruins. But by mid-November, the Russians gained the upper hand. The Soviets had nearly surrounded the 250,000 German troops. The battle continued for two months. On February 2, 1943, the German army finally surrendered.

America at War

In the Pacific, the Japanese were on the move. In 1940, Japan joined Italy and Germany as part of the Axis alliance. In July 1941, Japan invaded French Indochina. The United States stopped sending oil to Japan in response.

Japanese and U.S. officials met to discuss peaceful solutions. Yet, Japanese Admiral Isoroku Yamamoto had a secret plan to destroy the U.S. Pacific naval fleet based in Pearl Harbor, Hawaii. Yamamoto launched his surprise attack against U.S. forces on December 7, 1941, at 7:55 A.M. The Japanese unleashed 353 airplanes from six aircraft carriers in the Pacific Ocean. Bombs and torpedoes rained down on the unsuspecting U.S. fleet.

"This Is No Drill"

In Washington, D.C., a ringing telephone interrupted President Roosevelt, who was speaking with his military adviser Harry Hopkins. Secretary of the Navy Frank Knox was on the line. Knox told the president that he had received an urgent message from Pearl Harbor. The message said, "AIR RAID PEARL HARBOR . . . This is no drill."

Pearl Harbor comes under attack.

Destruction and Declaration

Five torpedoes ripped through the side of the battleship USS *Oklahoma*. Hundreds of sailors were trapped below the decks. The battleship USS *Arizona* blew up and sank in the harbor, killing 1,177 servicemen on board. More than 2,300 Americans were killed that day. The next day, President Franklin Roosevelt went before Congress to ask for a declaration of war.

"The American people in their righteous might will win through to absolute victory," said Roosevelt. An anxious nation listened to their radios. Congress declared war against Japan the following day. Germany and Italy declared war on the United States on December 11th and vowed to defend their Japanese ally. On December 12th, the United States joined the war against the Axis powers.

Sleeping Giant

In response to the attack on Pearl Harbor, thousands of Americans joined the armed forces. The rest of America quickly got to work. Factories that had once made cars started producing tanks. School children collected scrap metal for America's factories. Women, who had not worked outside the home before the war, went to work to support the war effort. They made guns, bombs, tanks, and battleships.

While Americans **rationed** gasoline and **mobilized** in other ways, the war widened. In 1942, the Soviets were battling the Nazis alone on Europe's eastern front. The Soviets desperately wanted the United States and Britain to open a second front against Germany in the west. After much discussion, the United States and Great Britain attacked the Germans in Axis-occupied French North Africa.

▼ Women train at a Florida school so they can work for the war effort.

▲ Just two days before the invasion of Sicily, Allied artillery lines up.

Operation Torch

The Allies' plan was to push the Axis powers out of North Africa and gain control of the Mediterranean Sea. Controlling the Mediterranean would give the Allies many advantages.

The plan worked, but not immediately. The Allies had to battle German and Italian forces in Africa. In November 1942, the Allies surprised the Germans by invading Algeria and Morocco. The new American forces found out that they were not prepared to battle the seasoned Axis soldiers. Yet the American Army swiftly grew in confidence. In May 1943, the Axis forces were defeated in Africa.

▲ In California, workers inspect war-bound aircraft.

The Big Three

To defeat Germany, Japan, and Italy, the nations of Great Britain, the United States, and the Soviet Union began to work together, led by Winston Churchill, Franklin Roosevelt, and Joseph Stalin, respectively. These men were the leaders of the Allied forces and were known as the "Big Three."

Churchill, Stalin, and Roosevelt would meet face to face several times during the war to discuss how best to defeat the Axis powers. It was an uneasy alliance. Churchill and Roosevelt were leaders of the world's two greatest democracies. They were both distrustful of Stalin, who was a Communist. Churchill was especially unsure of the Soviets.

▶ Stalin, Roosevelt, and Churchill meet at the Tehran Conference in 1943.

Good Friends

Roosevelt and Churchill held meetings at the White House, at Roosevelt's Hyde Park, New York, home and in far-flung places such as Casablanca, Morocco, and Tehran, Iran. They became friends as a result. "It's fun to be in the same decade with you," Roosevelt once told Churchill.

Unconditional Surrender

Roosevelt was the first U.S. president to leave the country at a time of war. In January 1943, he and Churchill met in Morocco. Though Stalin was not present, they agreed that the Allies had to defeat Germany. The United States and Britain would refuse to negotiate a peace settlement. Only Germany's unconditional surrender would end the war.

Invasion of Italy

Once North Africa was under Allied control, the British and Americans decided to invade Sicily and the Italian mainland. Victory was achieved quickly on the Italian island of Sicily, but the fighting in Italy was long and hard.

In September 1943, the British crossed from Sicily to the Italian peninsula. The troops moved up from the "toe" of the Italian boot and up the eastern coast of the peninsula along the Adriatic Sea. That same month, U.S. troops landed at Salerno and moved northward toward Rome. In January 1944, more American soldiers landed in Anzio, a seaside town on the Mediterranean coast.

▲ In 1944, U.S. Sherman tanks head to battle in Anzio, Italy.

Gustav Line

The Italian army surrendered to Allied forces as the Germans retreated and formed the Gustav Line. The Gustav Line was a defensive position stretching across Italy south of Rome. Moreover, the winter of 1943–1944 was the worst Italy had seen in years. The weather hampered the ability of the Allies to push northward.

Cold and mud slowed the Allied advance to Rome. It took four tries between January and May 1944 before the Allies broke through the German lines. Rome finally fell to the Allies on June 4, 1944. The Allies had gained an important foothold in southern Europe.

▲ The Allied invasion of Sicily begins.

● The March to Rome

1 British troops cross from Sicily to the Italian mainland.

2 American forces land at Salerno in September of 1943.

3 American troops storm the beaches near Anzio and begin a slow, deadly march to Rome.

4 Rome falls in June of 1944.

Key Events

⇢	U.S. Advances with Dates
⇢	British Advances with Dates
—	Major German Defensive Lines

SWITZERLAND · AUSTRIA
Milan · Verona · Venice
Trieste 1945 · MAY 1945
Padua · APRIL 1945
YUGOSLAVIA
Genoa · Rimini
Gothic Line
Florence
ITALY
Corsica · Rome · Gustav Line
June 1944 · Cassino
Anzio · Foggia
Naples
Occupied by free French September, 1943 · Salerno
Sardinia · Taranto
January 1944 · September 1943
N
Palermo · Messina
Mediterranean Sea · Sicily · Reggio di Calabria
0   100 miles Gela · Siracuse
100 km

In the Pacific

While fighting raged in Africa and Italy, the war in the Pacific was also heating up. Guam, New Guinea, the Solomon Islands, and the Philippines had fallen to the Japanese.

The Philippines

The Philippines was the most discouraging loss for the Americans. American and Filipino forces were sick and hungry. They defended the Philippine islands as best they could, but they finally had to surrender on April 9, 1942. The Japanese captured almost 78,000 Allied troops. The Japanese forced their prisoners to march to a prison camp. Along the way, many U.S. and Filipino soldiers died.

▲ The airfield on Eastern Island, in the Philippines, comes under attack.

◄ Oil tanks burn on Sand Island, in the Philippines.

Island Hopping

U.S. General Douglas MacArthur and Admiral Chester Nimitz came up with a plan called "island hopping" to beat the Japanese. The **strategy** called for American troops to attack and occupy one island after another across the Pacific all the way to Japan. The Americans hit their enemy at its weakest points. Using this strategy, the Americans won decisive battles at Tarawa, Guadalcanal, and other islands.

Midway Island

In June 1942, the Japanese took aim at Midway Island, a tiny atoll in the Pacific about 1,000 miles (1,609 km) northwest of Hawaii. Japan wanted to force U.S. carriers into the open and destroy them. Instead, the Americans broke a secret Japanese code and discovered Japan's plans. The U.S. immediately attacked the Japanese fleet. After Midway, the Japanese navy never recovered. From then on, America was on the offensive in the Pacific.

On to Berlin

Hitler believed that after five years of fighting, Germany still could defeat the Allies. However, the Soviets continued to press on them from the east, and Allied forces were moving toward them from Italy. The Allies secretly prepared to invade Western Europe through France.

The Allied invasion of Europe began on June 6, 1944, which is known as D-Day. Allied planners secretly assembled the greatest naval invasion force ever. In a risky crossing of the English Channel, Allied troops headed for the beaches of Normandy, France. It was an unexpected place to attack, so Hitler believed it was a **diversion**. He thought the main invasion would come from elsewhere. Within days, thousands of Allied forces were moving across France. By late 1944, the Allies were marching across Belgium, too.

D-Day Numbers

By nightfall of the first day, 130,000 troops were ashore. Although Allied casualties were high, they had successfully begun Europe's **liberation.** Eventually, more than 2,800,000 Allied soldiers, sailors, and airmen would be in Europe.

▲ U.S. troops reach Omaha Beach, a code name for one of the five landing spots.

◀ On Utah Beach, the troops go into battle.

Battle of the Bulge

On December 16, 1944, Hitler ordered a surprise counterattack. His plan called for 1,000 tanks and other weapons. Germans charged through the snow-covered Ardennes Forest. The Germans pushed back a section of the Allied front lines. The Battle of the Bulge had begun. The shocked Allies retreated but did not surrender. The weather was freezing cold, which grounded the Allied planes. The counterattack seemed to be working for the Germans. Then, the German tanks ran out of gas.

By late January 1945, the Germans retreated. More than 100,000 Germans died or were wounded. Allied casualties totaled 80,000. It was the last great German offensive of World War II.

The Final Battle

As the Americans and British moved toward Berlin from the west and north, the Soviets squeezed Nazi Germany from the east. By April 1, 1945, the Russians were just outside Berlin.

By the time the Soviets reached the Nazi capital, Berlin was already in ruins. British and American bombers had flown over Berlin for years, dropping thousands of bombs on the city. Expecting the worst, however, the Soviets massed troops and equipment on the outskirts of the city for two weeks. They believed the Nazis would fight to the death to protect their beloved capital.

► The Soviets defend the streets of Stalingrad before going on the offense in Berlin.

▼ The German Reichstag burns.

Surrounded

On April 16, the Russian armies closed in on Berlin from the north, west, and south. Within days, some 2.5 million troops had surrounded the city. The Nazis had been preparing for a **siege** since January, but their preparations were not enough to stop Soviet troops.

On April 20, Hitler's birthday, Soviet artillery began shelling the center of the city. On April 21, 1945, *The New York Times* reported that the "Battle for Berlin is in full swing."

"From the east and the northeast the Russians are rolling relentlessly down on the German capital, whose burning towers have been in sight for several days. The outer defenses of the city already are said to have been overrun."

A day later, Adolf Hitler still declared that the war was not lost. As he hid in a bunker below the ground, 300,000 German soldiers defended the city. The Allied bombardment did not stop until the Nazis surrendered on May 2, 1945.

End in Europe

The end of the war was in sight. U.S. President Franklin Roosevelt, British Prime Minister Winston Churchill, and Soviet leader Joseph Stalin met to decide Germany's postwar fate.

The Allied leaders met at Yalta and made a plan to divide Germany into occupied zones. The Soviets, British, Americans, and French would each control one zone after the war. At the same meeting, the Soviets agreed to enter the war against Japan in the Pacific.

In Germany, Hitler, his wife, and several other Nazi leaders committed suicide before they could be captured. They had been living in a secret Berlin bunker, named Fuhrerbunker. German General Weidling was left in charge, and he soon surrendered to the Allies. The terrible war in Europe was over.

▶ In London, people celebrate the end of the fighting.

In the Concentration Camps

As Allied soldiers moved into Nazi-held areas of Europe, they discovered the Nazi death camps. The Nazis had murdered between 9 million and 11 million innocent people. Inside the Nazi death camps, Jews and members of other groups targeted by the Nazis had been put to death in gas chambers. Others had been hanged or shot. Still others died of starvation while working as slaves.

The Allied forces were shocked by their discoveries. It was widely known that the Nazis used concentration camps to imprison political enemies and others. However, the horrors of the death camps were beyond belief.

The Allied troops liberated the surviving camp prisoners. The death camps themselves—Buchenwald, Auschwitz, Dachau, and others—are now museums to honor the victims of this human tragedy.

▼ Slave laborers are found in Buchenwald in 1945.

Iwo Jima

By early 1945, the Americans had taken back most of the territory conquered by the Japanese early in the war. The U.S. then focused its attention on an island called Iwo Jima, about 660 miles (1,062 km) south of Tokyo.

Iwo Jima was halfway between Tokyo and the American bomber bases in the Mariana Islands. Capturing the island would put the Americans within striking distance of the Japanese mainland.

Home Soil

The Japanese dug a series of fortified tunnels on Iwo Jima, which they considered home soil. Their orders were to fight to the death. The Japanese hoped that if they could kill and wound many American soldiers, the United States would think twice about launching another attack on Japanese land.

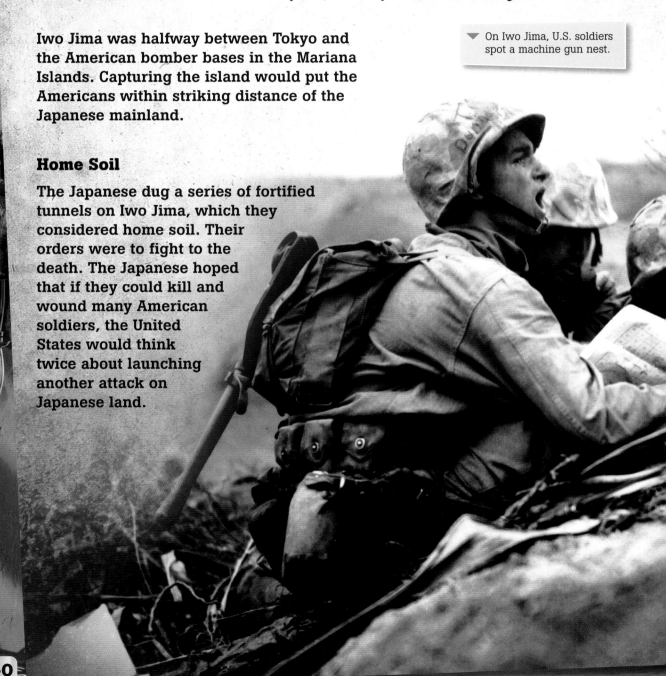

▼ On Iwo Jima, U.S. soldiers spot a machine gun nest.

Heavy Shelling

Early on February 19, U.S. bombers and battleships began bombing Iwo Jima. The huge guns blasted away at the tiny island and signaled the beginning of the invasion. However, the Japanese were hiding in their vast and heavily fortified tunnel network.

On the Beach

At around 9 A.M., the first U.S. Marines landed. The Japanese held their fire as the first wave of Marines hit the beaches. Most of the Americans thought that the heavy bombardment from the Navy ships had killed the Japanese. As the Americans tried to advance inland from the beaches, however, the Japanese opened fire, inflicting many American casualties with their machine-guns.

▲ Marines plant a U.S. flag on Suribachi.

Famous Photo

On February 23, a small group of Marines climbed to the top of Mount Suribachi and raised the American flag. A now-famous photograph was taken of these six Marines. It was the model for a statue that was created to commemorate those who died in the battle. The statue is in Arlington National Cemetery in Virginia. Three of the six men did not survive the fighting.

The battle on Iwo Jima ended in a Japanese defeat on March 26. About 6,821 Allied forces were killed in action, and thousands more were wounded or missing. It was the deadliest battle in U.S. Marine Corps history.

The Atomic Bomb

By the time Berlin fell, Harry S. Truman was the new U.S. president. Roosevelt had died on April 15, 1945. He did not live to see Hitler's defeat. Truman, the former vice president, took charge of the war against Japan, which continued even after Germany's surrender.

When Truman came to office, American scientists in New Mexico had already tested the world's first atomic bomb. The test bomb demonstrated never-before-seen destructive power. U.S. scientists prepared two atomic bombs that could be used against enemies. The scientists nicknamed the two bombs "Fat Man" and "Little Boy."

▶ The U.S. atomic bomb drops on Hiroshima, Japan.

Forcing Surrender

On August 6, 1945, a U.S. B-29 bomber dropped the first atomic bomb, "Little Boy," on Hiroshima, Japan. A mushroom cloud of smoke rose above the city. About 70,000 people were killed immediately. Three days later, the Americans dropped the second bomb, "Fat Man," on Nagasaki, Japan. On August 14th, Emperor Hirohito announced Japan's unconditional surrender.

End of the War

The end of the war in the Pacific formally came on September 2, 1945. The Japanese minister of foreign affairs signed papers of surrender. The greatest conflict in human history was finally over.

▼ Japanese officials get ready to sign surrender papers.

New World Order

The United States and the Soviet Union emerged from World War II as the world's superpowers.

United Nations

After WWII, the Allies set up the United Nations (UN) to try to settle quarrels between countries and avoid future wars. World War II had forced the United States to end its **isolationism**. Members of the UN hoped that all countries had learned the lessons of WWII.

After the war, the United States helped rebuild a shattered Europe, including Germany, and a broken Japan. However, the U.S. and the Soviet Union stopped being allies and became adversaries.

The Soviets controlled East Germany. France, Britain, and the United States controlled West Germany. An **ideological** struggle arose between the United States and the Soviet Union.

After Germany's surrender, the U.S. wanted to stop the Communists from moving into other countries. Although the two nations never fought directly on a battlefield, the U.S. and the Soviet Union formed military alliances with other nations. Historians call this struggle the Cold War. The Cold War was fought without bombs or bullets.

Proxy Wars

The Americans and Soviets had other countries fight smaller **proxy** wars so they did not have to face one another on the battlefield. The Americans and Soviets competed against one another in sports, in spying, and in the race to the moon.

Lessons Learned?

The Soviet Union collapsed in the 1990s. The United States became friends with the countries that had made up the Soviet Union, including Russia. Today, the influences of World War II continue to affect the nations of the world, which are still trying to learn from its lessons.

▼ An Allied road convoy arrives in Berlin in 1949.

▼ The United States delivers supplies to Berlin after the war.

Timeline

Major Dates in World War II (1939–1945)

1939

September 1, 1939: Germany invades Poland.

September 3, 1939: France and Britain declare war against Germany.

September 28, 1939: Poland surrenders.

1940

May 1940: Nazis conquer Luxembourg, Netherlands, and Belgium.

June 4, 1940: The British and French evacuation of Dunkirk ends.

June 14, 1940: Paris falls.

1941

June 22, 1941: Germany invades the Soviet Union.

December 7, 1941: Japan attacks the U.S. Fleet based in Pearl Harbor, Hawaii. The U.S. declares war the next day.

December 11, 1941: U.S. declares war on Germany and Italy.

1942

April 9, 1942: Philippines falls to Japan.

1943

July 10, 1943: Allies invade Sicily.

1944

June 6, 1944: Allies invade Normandy, France.

December 16, 1944: Battle of the Bulge begins.

1945

May 7, 1945: Germany surrenders.

August 6, 1945: U.S. drops atomic bomb on Hiroshima, Japan.

August 9, 1945: U.S. drops second atomic bomb on Nagasaki, Japan.

August 14, 1945: Japan surrenders.

Glossary

alliance—a group that forms to help one another

appeasement—an attempt to maintain peace by giving in to someone's demands

armistice—when war is stopped by agreement from both sides

annex—to add a territory into one's own territory

compromise—a settlement in which each side gives up something

destroyers—small, fast warships

diversion—a plan used to distract an enemy from a real attack

ideological—relating to a set of beliefs of a particular individual or group

isolationism—holding back from political or economic relations with other countries

juggernaut—a force too powerful to stop

liberation—freedom; freeing people or a nation from imprisonment or occupation

mobilized—assembled and made ready, as for war

neutral—not wanting to take part in something, as in a war between countries

proxy—the power to act for another

rationed—used in controlled amounts, often for purposes of conserving resources

reparations—payments to repair a past harm

repressive—controlling or holding down or back

siege—a military action in which a place is surrounded in order to force its surrender

strategy—a military plan

Further Reading

Adams, Simon. *World War II* (DK Eyewitness Books). New York: DK Publishing, 2007.

Provost Beller, Susan. *Battling in the Pacific: Soldering in World War II.* Minneapolis, MN: Twenty-First Century Books, 2008.

Graham, Ian (author); David Antram (illustrator). *You Wouldn't Want to Be a World War II Pilot!* New York: Scholastic, 2007.

Makanaoalani Nicholson, Dordina. *Remember World War II: Kids Who Survived Tell Their Stories*. Washington, D.C.: National Geographic Children's Books, 2005.

Ask your parents to help you research more about World War II on the Internet.